John Knowles OBE with Tiggy.

INTRODUCTION

When writing this book, I soon realised that the story of Marwell was to be no ordinary account about the opening of a zoo. Firstly there was the rich history of Marwell Hall and the estate that surrounds it. Space permits only a brief summary here to cover a period of one thousand years, leaving many fascinating topics for future research. Secondly, there was the story of the creation of Marwell Zoological Park.

I had been fortunate enough to become involved with Marwell from its early days, and remember the fields of rolling countryside before they became familiar to the gentle grunts from the herds of oryx and the splash of tigers playing in their pools. This book is as much about ideals and understanding, conservation and international co-operation, as it is about managing animals in captivity. During the twenty-one years since Marwell first opened its gates to the public, there have been many dramatic changes in the outside world, with inevitable impact on many wild animal populations. There have also been dramatic changes in the zoo community, and no small part, in these changes of attitude and responsibility, has been due to the example of the founder, and Director, of Marwell Zoological Park, John Knowles, OBE.

The role of captive-breeding programmes has become the lifeline for many species, and is accepted as a valuable contribution towards the complex needs of wildlife conservation. It is likely to be a long time before the vital work being undertaken by progressive zoos becomes unnecessary. This will only happen when mankind stops destroying the natural resources of the world and learns to live in harmony with wildlife and wild places. Until then, good zoos, such as Marwell Zoological Park, deserve all the help that they can get.

John L. Adams

Marwell Hall.

CHAPTER ONE

THE HISTORY OF THE ESTATE AND MARWELL HALL

The history of Marwell goes back long before the building of Marwell Hall, indeed the name 'Merewell', as it was originally called, can be traced back over one thousand years. The name comes from two words, 'mere', meaning a pool or lake, and 'well', referring to a spring or source of water. The present Marwell Zoological Park has no natural bodies of water; the nearest natural lake is Fisher's Pond located about a mile away. There are, however, a number of natural springs around the Zoo, and a borehole can supply plenty of good quality water from underground.

During the reign of the Anglo-Saxon King, Eldred, Merewell was given to the new monastery in Winchester, thus establishing what was to become an important link with the City of Winchester, which was then the capital of England. Merewell was given 'with thirty hides' – a hide being a measure of land equivalent to 120 acres – to the monastery, which was later to be called Hyde Abbey, the ruins of which remain today. In 964, King Eadgar the Peaceful granted lands in Owslebury (which is Marwell's parish village) to the Bishop of Winchester, including the land that is now Marwell Zoological Park.

Marwell is not listed in the Domesday Book by name, but it is assumed that it appears as the unnamed manor under the two Twyford entries of land belonging to the Bishop of Winchester. This is described to be held by 'Alded, Oswald's wife.' The manor held seventeen villagers and twenty smallholders with seven ploughs; three slaves; two mills valued at £5 15*s.* and thirty-two acres of meadow. The value placed on the manor at the time of the survey was £12 and, by the time that the Domesday Book was published about twenty years later in 1086, the value was increased to £15.

The Bishop of Winchester, Henry de Blois, founded a small college of secular priests at Marwell and a palace at Marwell Manor, during the period of 1129 to 1171. He also founded the first hospital at St. Cross in Winchester. Marwell Manor must not be confused with Marwell Hall, which stands at the heart of Marwell Zoological Park. The present Marwell Manor is located close to the Zoo on the main road between Bishop's Waltham and Winchester, and it was on this site that the palace stood. The moated enclosure around the palace remains today. The task of the priests was to pray for the souls of the King of England and for the Bishops of Winchester, for which they received the sum of sixty shillings a year, of which twenty shillings were to be spent on the lighting and ornaments in the church. The palace is thought to have fallen into ruin in the 16th century and it is believed that the majority of the remains were removed at the beginning of the 19th century to build Shawford House, a building a few miles to the north-west.

Royal connections were first forged by the visit of Henry II to Merewell to meet Henry de Blois before the King sailed from Portsmouth to France in 1170 and, in 1186, de Blois' successor as Bishop of Winchester, Toclyve, received Henry II again at Merewell.

Although ancient woodland remains around Marwell today, and is protected, the extent of woodland in the middle ages was far greater. Timber was a valuable resource, particularly in demand for dwellings and ship-building. In 1280 an order was issued to William de Hamilton, guardian of the bishopric of Winchester, for the immediate delivery of five oaks from the park of Merewell for use for the works of St. Swithun's Priory. St. Swithun's Priory was later to become Winchester Cathedral.

In 1284, Edward I gave up all of his rights in the manor of Twyford with Marwell (the name by which this manor of Owslebury was known) to the Bishop of Winchester, John de Pontissar, and the bishop's successors. It was during this period that Marwell Hall was built. In 1305, Henry Woodlock de Merewelle became the Bishop of Winchester, and the area became known as Marwell Woodlock. It was possibly Henry Woodlock who built the original hall. The Manor of Marwell was purchased by Bishop Fox of Winchester in 1518 and he gave it, together with lands around Owslebury – including that which is now Marwell Zoological Park – to the Corpus Christi College, Oxford, which he had founded a few years before. The land was leased out by the college until it passed into the possession of the Crown in 1551. However, the Lordship of Marwell Woodlock

Back garden of the Hall before the Zoo was developed.

remained with the college until they decided to put the title up for sale by auction in 1987. Mrs. Jacqueline Lodge, who was already a member of the Marwell Zoological Society and an animal adopter, spotted that the auction was to take place and purchased the title, thus ensuring that the Lordship of Marwell Woodlock was back within the Marwell domain, albeit some 470 years later.

The changes caused by the dissolution of the monasteries in 1538 brought about renewed royal connections. A condition of the appointment of John Poynet to the see of Winchester was that he should surrender all of the episcopal munros in exchange for a fixed income of 2,000 marks, which was why Corpus Christi College lost Marwell to the Crown thirteen years later. It was then that the Chantry of Marwell, with appurtenances, was granted to Sir Henry Seymour, and Marwell was restored by Queen Mary to the bishopric of Winchester. The Seymour family is said to have leased the manor previously, and the family continued to live at Marwell for three generations. Memorials on the surviving carved oak mantelpiece in Marwell Hall show the paternal coat of Seymour and the Seymour crest – a flaming phoenix in ducal coronet. Much of the Hall was rebuilt during the Seymour period of occupation. Tradition has it that Henry VIII secretly married Jane Seymour – Sir Henry's sister – in a first-floor room of Marwell Hall on the day that Anne Boleyn was executed, although this seems most unlikely, as the Hall was not in the possession of the Seymours at the time.

Jane Seymour's son, Edward VI, is believed to have stayed in the Hall during his journey through Surrey, Sussex and Hampshire in search of health in 1552, the year before he died, and his coat of arms can be seen over the stone fireplace in the Hall today. It was perhaps fitting that John Knowles, Director of the Zoo, should have been educated at the King Edward's School, in Chelmsford, which was one of the schools that Edward VI had established around Britain during his reign.

In the seventeenth century the Hall passed into the hands of Sir Henry Mildmay who was a favourite of Charles I, although he later defected to the Parliamentarian cause. He lived at Marwell during the Civil War and, in 1644, while a troop of sixty men were quartered at Marwell, there was a skirmish between the Parliamentarians and a party of some two hundred Cavaliers, who were a little the worse for drink! Some of the Cavaliers were killed, and others were captured.

In the late seventeenth century, King Charles II is said to have visited Marwell frequently – he was a friend of Major Richard Brett who had bought Marwell in 1679. Major Brett had two daughters, one of whom had married a Mr. Darce. Their son, Ranulph Darce, left Marwell to join the navy and served in the 1812 war against America. He resigned from the navy three years later and went into merchant trading, which brought him eventually to New Zealand. The great, great grandson of Ranulph Darce still lives in New Zealand and he returned to visit his ancestral home in 1986 – and became a share adopter of a Przewalski horse in the Zoo.

There is rumour of a fire at Marwell in the early 19th century which was said to have destroyed much of the original Hall. However, there is no firm evidence of this. What is known is that in 1816, the then owner, William Long, completed extensive rebuilding of the Hall, having found it 'in a dilapidated state'. His rebuilding is how the Hall appears today, with little of the original structure showing apart for the two fireplaces previously mentioned, parts of the floors and cellars and, interestingly, the structure of the roof.

In recent years the Marwell Preservation Trust, with the assistance of grants from English Heritage, Winchester City and Hampshire County Councils, has spent considerable sums on the repair and preservation of the Hall, which is a Grade I listed building. Much of the work has been concerned with the roof, where investigation of the timbers established that the structure was medieval, and therefore the Hall was built much earlier than in the Tudor period, as had been previously supposed. The 'base-cruck' structure of the roof beams probably dates the Hall to the first half of the 14th century. Although the roof structure remains, it cannot be seen by visitors as it is obscured by a plaster vaulted ceiling which was built in the 19th century. The original Hall would have been open to expose the roof beams, with a central turret to let smoke out from the open fire. The fact that the timbers were smoke-blackened by this central hearth, and that they were otherwise in sound condition, was further evidence that the hall had not been burnt down prior to the alterations made in the early part of the last century.

In 1845 John Gully moved into the Hall. He was a remarkable man who had survived, but lost, a sixty-four round boxing match held in Bristol in the days before the Queensbury Rules were introduced, but that earned him the respect that built an early career as a prize-fighter. After retiring from boxing he went into horse racing and trained horses at Danebury in Hampshire although not, to our knowledge, at Marwell. He married twice, had twenty-four children and eventually became MP for Pontefract.

Pony club rally held in the Park in 1970.

Many famous people reputedly stayed at Marwell, including George Romney, the 19th-century portrait painter, whose reputation was on the level of Reynolds and Gainsborough. An octagonal room was specially converted for artists on the first floor of the Hall, with the unusual incorporation of a large window immediately above the mantelpiece in order to achieve plenty of northern daylight into the room. Today the room is appropriately used by the Zoo's graphic artist. Sir Alfred Tennyson also stayed in the Hall and played cricket for the Marwell XI.

The Hall passed into the hands of the Standish family, and a number of generations occupied the house between 1867 and 1933.

During World War II, Mr. and Mrs. Hayes lived in the Hall, and the grounds of Marwell and the surrounding area were used as an airfield for fighter aircraft from 1941. Mr. Hayes was the Managing Director of the Cuncliffe Owen Aircraft Factory in Swaythling, near Southampton. Planes were flown in, usually by women pilots, from factories throughout the county, prior to going into service. Trees made a natural camouflage, and by joining fields together, cutting gaps in hedges and closing the main road, a satisfactory runway was established. Some of the hangars used remain today on the farmland adjacent to the Zoo. The Hall had been used for staff accommodation, and writing on the wall in part of the cellars suggest that parties had occured from time to time as a relief from the pressures of the War! Mrs. Hayes used to invite WI members from Owslebury over to the Hall, where they met to make jam in the kitchen and knit garments for the troops.

It is hardly surprising that a building with the history of Marwell should have its share of ghost stories. Jane Seymour is said to haunt the corridors of the Hall and Anne Boleyn haunts the ancient Yew Walk behind the Hall, waiting to wreak her vengeance on Jane Seymour. Neither tale is supported by the fact that the Seymours did not possess the Hall at the time of Anne's death or Jane's wedding in 1536. The ghost of the Yew Walk is thought by some to be the spirit of another person, as indeed was the 'presence' that used to regularly stop the oilman's horse when walking past the gates to the Hall at night.

The best-known legend is that of the 'mistle bough bride'. A young bride, weary of dancing on the night of her Christmastide wedding, hid herself in an old oak chest, only to discover that the spring-lock would not permit her escape and that the heavy chest muffled her cries for help. When her body was discovered many years later, a sprig of mistletoe was by her side. It is said that around 11 o'clock on the night after Boxing Day, the sounds of the crowd of young wedding guests can be heard rushing along the corridors of Marwell Hall. The story prompted Thomas Bayly (1823 to 1877) to write a ballad *The Mistletoe Bough*. The tale, however, is said to originate from other houses too, including one in Bramshill, also in Hampshire. As some evidence in Marwell's favour, the chest was reported to have remained in the Hall until the mid-19th century before being removed to the rectory at nearby Upham, where the Rector used to delight in showing it to visitors. The chest, though, has long since vanished.

Another ghostly story is of nocturnal bumps and sounds heard in one of the bedrooms. The cause was reputed to be the noises of barrels and cases of contraband being dragged across the floor of a secret passage when being moved to their storage place in the chimney of the room. A doorway in the room led to 'a fairly secret stairway', although no evidence of this stairway exists today.

East face of the Hall.

One fact though, was that Sir Henry Seymour was no lover of the Roman Catholics and his hatred of the Popery came to a head when he dragged a priest from the parish church and had him shot dead. The priest was to have already cursed Sir Henry, and all his kin, by 'bell, book and candle', and legend has it that owners of Marwell will not long occupy the property. Certainly the Seymours resided at Marwell for only three generations, and luck has not been on the side of some subsequent owners. This century, one burnt to death in a blazing car in the 1930s, another ended his days facing financial ruin, and a third managed to get shot in the foot during a hunting accident. Perhaps there was additional wisdom in John Knowles transferring the ownership of Marwell Hall to the Marwell Preservation Trust or, perhaps, like the ravens in the Tower of London, the presence of the animals at Marwell have laid the ghosts to rest.

Summer 1970, John Knowles with the Przewalski horses.

CHAPTER TWO

THE CREATION OF THE ZOO

In the mid-1960s a successful English businessman stopped in a bar in Boston, Massachusetts for a break before travelling on to visit his company's US head office. He got into conversation with a man who turned out to be Walter D. Stone, Director of two zoos in the State – the Franklin Park Zoo in Boston, and the Middlesex Fells Zoo in Stoneham. The conversation proved to be the turning point in the life of the businessman, as he was John Knowles and the conversation indirectly led him to create Marwell Zoological Park.

Walter D. Stone took John to meet some friends, the Lindemann's, who ran the Catskill Game Farm, in upstate New York. John Knowles and Roland Lindemann got on famously and established a friendship that would lead to Catskill animals being in the foundation stock at Marwell. It was while staying at Catskill that John Knowles was allowed to clean out the off-exhibit group of Przewalski horses. There was something about these rare animals that struck an immediate chord in his heart and mind, and the future began to take shape. The Catskill

Game Farm was an esoteric collection located in beautiful rocky countryside, with a remarkable collection of ungulates – the hoofed animals that were to also become Marwell's speciality. It was not to be many years later that Przewalski horses were amongst the early arrivals for the embryo Zoo. It was not, however, from Catskill, nor indeed Boston, that the first animals were purchased for Marwell, nor were they ungulates; their story comes later.

'Tiger Junction' as it was in May 1971.

John Knowles was born in Chelmsford, Essex, the only child of Frank and Florence Knowles. His father was Head of the Department of Agricultural Chemistry at the Essex Institute of Agriculture. Despite the austerity of a childhood during the War years, John developed a liking for animals and kept mice, rabbits, guinea pigs and stick insects. There was, too, the excitement of visits to London Zoo and Whipsnade Park, where the elephants, in particular, made a formidable impression to the extent that the thought occured to him of becoming an elephant keeper. Childhood dreams seldom come true – at least not quite as perceived through a child's eyes.

Tiger enclosure under construction, 1971.

He attended the King Edward VI Grammar School in Chelmsford, which he admits he did not enjoy and which, in hindsight, certainly underestimated the potential of this particular pupil. He took from school a deep and enduring love of English and English literature, but otherwise had little fond memories of school life; more frequently ending up in detention than achieving merit.

After school he graduated at the Essex Agricultural Institute. A career in farming seemed the only, rather bleak, prospect and so, with some experience of farm work under his belt, and with the raw materials of an unpromising small and derelict farm, he worked hard in a period of post-war rationing and constraint, eventually specialising in poultry breeding. As this dour period passed, and as more people began to enjoy some luxuries such as chicken, his business began to flourish. Links with a colleague in Norfolk, and a successful American company, marked an important change in John's life.

The American poultry market had not suffered from the feedstuff rationing that had occured in Britain, and their stock was better. Marketing this good breeding stock worldwide was suddenly John's responsibility and this meant travel, particularly in developing countries where John saw not only the wildlife of many continents but also, at first hand, the conflicts between man and animals. A memorable example of this was the depredations made by elephants in the sugar cane plantations of Ceylon – now Sri Lanka – and the extermination of these magnificent animals as the local farmers' solution to this threat to their livelihoods.

John became a successful businessman, married with two sons, and apparently, settled. There was, however, the thought in the back of his mind that, despite his commercial successes, there was the sense of a lack of fulfilment. The chance meeting in Boston had been the catalyst needed to break away from the relative security of his lifestyle, and accept the challenge of his true vocation in life – of creating Britain's first zoological collection specifically for the breeding of endangered animal species, and implementing many innovative changes to the operations of zoological gardens and animal conservation.

In the 1960s zoos were proliferating world-wide and in Britain, as elsewhere, the leisure industry had grown as more people had more disposable income. In 1966 the first Safari Park opened at Longleat and it was soon to be followed by others including those at Windsor, Woburn and Knowsley. Then dolphins became a craze, with dozens of places, many of them unsuitable, exhibiting these intelligent mammals in the early 1970s. The British zoo boom peaked with well over a hundred and thirty collections. Many of these were poor places, led by commercial interests and with no real purpose other than that of entertainment. Marwell was to be different, and Marwell has remained loyal to this promise, witnessed dramatic changes in the zoo community and the enlightenment of a fair sector of the public.

March 1972 and the roads are still being constructed! The giraffe house is on the hill.

John Knowles considered his ideas for the Zoological Park and made initial enquiries to find a suitable site. The first place that he looked at was near Salisbury. This had several attractive features, but it was not a particularly

Boris and Lena, the first animals to arrive at Marwell, in the stable yard.

good catchment area for visitors, and the close proximity to Longleat Safari Park was also not in its favour. Marwell, which had only recently been placed on the market, was only the second place he looked at and, while the estate had a number of advantages, there was the lack of natural water. There would be plenty of time to look at other places when he returned from his next business trip to the United States – or so John Knowles thought at the time.

In February 1969 he found himself in Florida after a business trip to the eastern coast of the USA. He visited the Rare Feline Breeding Center at Center Hill, as he had heard that they kept many zoo rarities including black jaguar, maned wolves and Siberian tigers. He was shown around the collection, and introduced to a beautiful pair of two-year-old Siberian tigers called Boris and Lena. The owner expressed his regret that John Knowles's plans for his zoo were not further advanced as the tigers were available but may be purchased soon by an American zoo. That was all it took for John Knowles to ask the dealer not to sell the tigers until he had the chance to get back to England, and bring forward his plans. Suddenly he had found himself the proud owner of two of the world's treasures; the formulation of a zoological park in his mind and the ideals of captive breeding to aid the conservation of animals – but nowhere to achieve it! The pressure was suddenly on, and John Knowles made an urgent telephone call to his estate agent to go ahead and purchase the property in Hampshire.

Marwell Hall, and the surrounding 417 acres of land, was purchased on the 29th September 1969. John Knowles moved into the Hall, little realising the pending problems that would be encountered before the zoo could be opened. The Hall was to remain his home – initially using two floors, and then the first floor when the Zoo opened, until moving out in 1980 to make room for the offices, Education Centre and other activities of the Marwell Preservation Trust.

Prior to the opening of the Zoo, one of the fundamental requirements was to obtain animals. At that time the importation of animals from the wild was more frequent than it is today, but the majority of the original stock was captive-bred, although some animals from the wild would be critical to the breeding potential of the animals that were to become Marwell's specialities.

The period saw a number of significant changes in the laws that controlled the importation, and exportation, of animals and, while these were ultimately beneficial and desirable, their imposition created further complications and escalated costs. There was the threat looming of a rabies scare which could have resulted in a complete ban on the importation of cats, so priority was given to get the tigers, and other big cats, into the country as soon as possible. The ban lasted for only a short time, but the consequent Rabies Act was introduced which controlled a far wider group of animals than just the carnivores – from rodents to primates. All these animals had to undergo a strictly controlled quarantine period of six months and, although Marwell later met the Ministry of Agriculture and Fisheries standards to allow rabies quarantine in the Park, places had to be found to quarantine the first carnivores elsewhere. Even more arduous was the need for almost all hoofed stock to undergo a year's quarantine in an urban situation. The associated management, feeding, veterinary, transportation and inspection costs would be an added burden on the early finances of Marwell.

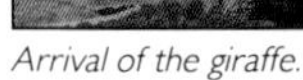
Arrival of the giraffe.

Release of the hog deer. Left to right: *Bill Oliver, Barry Hill, John Knowles and Martin Banks.*

The biggest blow, however, was in obtaining permission to open the Zoo, as the reaction from the local community had been underestimated. A stormy meeting was held in the local parish, at Owslebury Village Hall, on the 15th July 1969, and the room was so crowded that not only was it difficult to hear what was going on, but many people were unable to raise their opinions. It says a great deal for John Knowles that his intention to create a breeding sanctuary for endangered species was largely accepted by the community, and praised; their main concern was the likely impact of road traffic and disturbance, both from the traffic and the animals. There was also concern about the risk of animals escaping – a fear that was to prove groundless, but understandable, considering some of the events that had occured elsewhere.

It was agreed that a larger venue had to be found for a Public Meeting, and this was held at Ashburton Lodge, in Winchester, on the 11th September 1969 and was attended by almost 300 people. The interest that the meeting generated resulted in national newspaper coverage. The local parish council, at their meeting in the previous month, had recorded only twenty-one in favour of the park, whereas 130 were against. Like so many good things in life, it seemed that most people approved, provided that it was not on their doorstep.

The major zoological collections in Britain had united to form the Federation of Zoological Gardens of Great Britain and Ireland, and their secretary, Geoffrey St. G. Schomberg, spoke at the Public Meeting as one of the few in favour of John Knowles's plans. Despite the concerns expressed at this meeting, the Hampshire Planning Authority approved the Zoological Park in principle – by a vote of twelve to eight – in January 1970, a decision based on the calculation that the increase in traffic caused by the Zoo would be minimal compared with the total projected traffic levels.

This apparent good news was not, however, long-lived for, on the 1st April, the Ministry of Housing and Local Government 'called in' the planning decision so that a public enquiry could be held. Thus began the long wait and preparation for the Enquiry that was not to be held until the beginning of November 1970. The Enquiry, at many times heated, listened to many objectors, and far fewer supporters – the latter including Geoffrey Schomberg and Philip Wayre, Director of the Norfolk Wildlife Park. The feeling at the end of the nine-day Enquiry was far from positive. John Knowles knew that he had animals held around the world whose fate was now dependent on the decision from the Minister of the Environment. After the Enquiry the Minister took over six months to make a decision. The public heard the result before John Knowles did! On Saturday 22nd May 1971, he read in the local newspaper, The *Southern Evening Echo*, that approval had been granted. It was then 'all systems go'!

Enclosures for white-tailed gnu on the left. The leopard house would be built on the site behind the tractor, 1972.

In theory, a year should have sufficed to develop the Zoo; in fact it proved a greater task than first envisaged to transform a hundred acres of rolling fields into paddocks and enclosures, with all the associated services and amenities.

Some animals were, by then, already at the Park, temporarily housed in existing buildings around the Hall. The first animals to arrive, on the 5th February 1970, were Boris and Lena, the Florida-born Siberian tigers. When John Knowles had purchased the tigers he

Clouded leopard.

knew hardly anyone personally in the British zoo community, so he experienced some difficulties in not only persuading them about his intentions of opening a zoological park but that he desperately needed accommodation for a pair of Siberian tigers. One who did listen though, was the then director of Dudley Zoo, Cyril Grace, who also operated a small zoo in Birmingham and this is where the first tigers where eventually quarantined before coming to Marwell. The next species to arrive at Marwell to be settled in the old stables, were Grévy zebra. Other cats followed including two pairs of leopards, European lynx and pairs of cheetah, jaguar, clouded leopards and leopard cat. The original tigers were joined later by a trio of young Siberian tigers, Kurten, Nimana and Amaga, that had been bred at Leipzig in East Germany.

Kurten, Nimana and Amaga in quarantine in the stable yard.

The first Przewalski horse for Marwell was Vedran, who arrived in England from Prague on the 12th June 1969 and he, with other Przewalski horses that followed soon after, were kept at Colchester Zoo before arriving at Marwell in early 1970.

With the arrival of further zebras during the year, the stable yard was bulging to capacity. The Przewalski horses, temporarily held in corrals and pens, with some of the mares in fields enclosed by ordinary stock fences, could at least be reaccommodated as these hardy animals required minimal protection. So the Przewalskis were the first animals to be 'permanently' quartered in the Park when they were released into a five-acre paddock in the spring of 1971. However it would not be possible to introduce more delicate animals, such as the antelope, until permission had been obtained to build suitable accommodation for them.

Immediately the result of the enquiry had been announced, planning commenced, and the construction work started in the August of 1971. The first of the animal houses to be built was for the scimitar-horned oryx, with a second building for Grévy zebra, both of which served a large, partly moated paddock in front of the Hall. John Knowles had been told by at least one leading zoo director that the plan to keep zebra, oryx and ostrich together would be 'impossible' but, determined to achieve his dream of seeing large mixed groups of animals, John Knowles persevered and the paddock proved a success from the start, and is still accommodating all three species.

It was a fundamental decision that Marwell should remain as parkland, with large paddocks for natural groups of animals wherever practical and, where greater security was necessary – as for the big cats – enclosures that considered the behavioural needs of the animals, whether it be water for the tigers to play in, trees for the leopards to climb or distant views for the cheetahs to observe. John Knowles called in James Benham, from Chelmsford, to design most of the zoo buildings, which were to be mainly timber, or timber clad, structures to blend in with the countryside setting. The fact that they achieved this aim through their outward simplicity belies the fact that their design was innovative and has been significant in the success with a number of species. The first important feature was that every ungulate house would have an adjacent outside 'hardstanding', comprising a fenced yard with a well-drained hard surface, as well as having access to a grass paddock. This meant that all animals could be given access to the fresh air throughout the year, even when conditions were not suitable for them to go into the paddocks, and the hard surface was crucial in keeping the animals' hooves in good condition and thus reducing the risks that occur when ungulates are kept too long on soft ground. This was the inspiration of John Knowles from having seen the good

Arrival of scimitar-horned oryx and waterbuck from Belle Vue.

state of the hoof-stock at Catskill. Catskill was built on such rocky terrain that soil had to be imported for landscaping, but it suited their animals fine. Another innovation was to give each zebra its own stall at night, much in the way that many domesticated horses are kept. This overcame the squabbling that can occur when zebra are kept together, and the animals quickly learnt to use their own stalls each night. It was no coincidence that Marwell had bred from all three species of zebra before the Park even opened its gates to the public.

The layout of the park roads and enclosures was planned by John Knowles and Geoffrey Schomberg, whose interest in zoos and employment with the Federation had caused him to visit many different collections. Two basic decisions were that, for an extra charge, cars should be allowed to drive around the Park, and that the animals would be grouped in zoo-geographic zones. Today the layout of the roads and enclosures works well, but in the early days the animal exhibits were fairly sparsely scattered along the route around the Zoo. Some visitors, seeing that cars could be brought into the Park, presumed incorrectly that they were about to enter a 'drive-through' safari park.

The zoo-geographic zones were a brave idea, that has not often been achieved. The park was designed with a three-paddock African area; an Asian area to include, initially, the Przewalski horses, wild asses and tigers; a European area for lynx, tarpan and fallow deer; an American area for llama, guanaco, jaguar and rheas with, finally, an Australasian area for wallabies, emu and cassowary. The non-arrival of some intended species did not help, and it soon became apparent that the concept was too restrictive for practical animal management. The idea was phased out a few years after the park opened, although much of the African area still remains themed to the animals of that continent.

Marwell was to be no normal zoo. Its prime objective was to breed endangered species and to keep them, as far as practical, in natural groups. The main emphasis, initially at least, would be on the hoofed animals, with big cats as an important second. The selection of the initial, formative, groups of animals says much for John Knowles's insight and speculation at a time when the plight of many species in the wild was not fully appreciated. The stories of some of these – scimitar-horned oryx, Grévy zebra and Przewalski horse is told later. What is remarkable is, that at a time when many zoological gardens were fairly insular, and often possessive, John Knowles – who had, after all, no experience in the keeping of exotic animals – was not only listened to, but

Siberian tigers in their pool.

Lynx kittens, born in 1971, the first carnivores to be bred at Marwell.

accepted and entrusted with rare animals, many of which had been seldom kept, let alone bred, in Britain.

Since the first animals arrived, thousands have been born and hatched at Marwell. Their progeny have gone to breeding groups throughout the world, and some have become part of early reintroduction programmes for release of captive-bred animals back into the wild.

Throughout the chaotic period of establishing the Zoo, John Knowles had remained as joint Managing Director of the Anglian Food Group, and did not resign from that post until the future of the Zoo became reasonably secure. But that is moving the story on too fast . . .

One of the only pair of goral in the UK.

CHAPTER THREE

THE YEAR OF OPENING

The gates of Marwell Zoological Park opened to the public at 10.00 a.m. on Monday 22nd May 1972, exactly one year after the result of the Public Enquiry had been announced. The Enquiry had been a costly affair, and the delay that it caused through a period of inflation had been an unanticipated financial burden. It was critical to the establishment of the Park, which was estimated to have already cost £600,000, that some income was generated, if only to satisfy the, so far, tolerant manager of the National Westminster Bank. Had the preceding weather been more favourable, Marwell could have greeted its first visitors with a far better impression. As it was, May 22nd continued the weather scenario, albeit by being just a damp day rather than being a very wet one – but nevertheless, hardly conducive to seeing the Zoo at its best. The rain continued for the following month, with only two days of reasonable weather during

Grevy zebra and scimitar-horned oryx. The cedar of Lebanon, towering behind the Hall, was later to be damaged in gales.

thirty days. The public added to the quagmire of mud generated by the frantic building works and the laying of new water services that had been delayed by the previous bad weather.

they had probably never seen before in their lives for only 30p for adults, and 20p for children. So vouchers were also handed out to every visitor, giving them free entry for a return visit. In those days of innocence, the

Treetops Restaurant on the day the Zoo opened.

Opening day, with much work to be done on the South Road.

The result was that, apart from a few animal orientated people who could appreciate the concept beyond the mud, many early visitors were disillusioned and disappointed. What animals had been moved to permanent quarters were, quite sensibly, sheltering within buildings or on the far side of paddocks under the trees. Catering was conducted in a large marquee as the foundations for Treetops Restaurant had only just started. This marquee was located in part of a ploughed field that was later destined to become the first paddock encountered on entering the Zoo; unfortunately this also happened to be the lowest point in the Zoo and thus a natural draining point for the persistent rain. In consideration of the situation, the Park opened with reduced admission rates to those which had previously been set, and advertised, as 40p for adults and 25p for children. It soon became apparent that many visitors were still disappointed despite the fact that they could look at creatures that

vouchers had not been 'expiry dated', and they continued to filter back for years before it was discovered that the evolution of photocopiers had generated incoming vouchers that had never been issued by the Park!

Tom Murray and Reg Wareham were the first gatekeepers, and Tom had the distinction of selling the first admission ticket to Sam White, who headed the modest crowd who had been patiently queuing at the gate, avoiding the drizzle as much as possible. The late Sam White was one of the few people who stood up at the Enquiry in favour of John Knowles and, although he had been invited as a guest, he had been determined to be the first to buy a ticket. Tom Murray had been wearing a wide-brimmed hat to protect himself from the elements and, unbeknown to him, the brim had been steadily filling with water. As Tom bent over to issue a ticket, the water rolled out all over the unsuspecting customer; whether Sam White was the unfortunate recipient is not recorded!

On opening day, most of the paddocks, and many of the buildings, were unfinished. It was quite a long walk from the entrance kiosk to the first completed and occupied animal houses, those for cheetah and impala. The impala had proved particularly nervous animals and their enclosure fence had been screened with hessian to give these timid animals greater security. With some trepidation, the hessian on the front of the enclosure had been partly removed to allow a sight of these animals – then the only specimens in the UK. Although giraffe, nyala, the zebras, white-tailed gnu, waterbuck, blackbuck, goral, scimitar-horned oryx, Przewalski horses and tigers were amongst the animals permanently housed, it would be some weeks before others, such as the leopards, lynx, jaguar, flamingos, llamas, emus and rheas were similarly placed.

Leopard enclosure under construction, June 1972.

The activity on all fronts throughout the first season was frantic.

In addition to housing all of the animals already at Marwell, and completing enclosures and visitor facilities, animals continued to arrive from dealers and quarantine quarters, although two species intended for the Zoo and mentioned in the first guide book – red pandas and red kangaroos – failed to arrive. This was more than compensated by other newcomers that included a pair of Sumatran tigers from

Arrival of the Sumatran tigers; John Knowles looks on with Colin Hazzard in the background.

Rotterdam, Demoiselle and sarus cranes, emu bred at Belle Vue, Brazillian tapirs, Bennett's wallabies from the zoos of Jersey and Whipsnade, European bison and greater flamingos.

Not all arrivals were expected, though. One day the Zoo received a telephone call from the police in north Hampshire; they had captured a wild boar that had wandered into the police house gardens in Odiham. As the wild boar had long been extinct in Britain, and as there was no knowledge of anyone keeping boar in the area, Marwell thought that the animal may well turn out to be a domesticated pig. Nevertheless they travelled up to Odiham to take care of the capture. It was with some surprise that the animal was found to be a male wild boar, aged about two years, and he duly returned to Marwell and adopted the name Coulston, which, by strange coincidence happened to be the name of Marwell's local friendly police officer. Coulston was a character who loved his human visitors, but was destined to remain a bachelor as, despite a number of attempts to find him a mate, he twice killed females and a third, which managed to escape into adjacent woodland, had to be shot because of the risk of swine vesicular disease. It was never determined from whence Coulston originated, but he was almost certainly an escapee from a private collection, as a female wild boar was found victim of a road accident later in the year in the same vicinity. Coulston lived a long and contented life at Marwell.

Some animal arrivals, though, were short term visitors. The only other zoological collections in Hampshire at that time were the now long closed Chipperfield's operated Zoo on Southampton Common, and the Weyhill Zoo, near Andover, which has since evolved to become the Hawk Conservancy. Weyhill had a pair of sun bears, which had outgrown their accommodation and were proving, as bears often do, to be quite destructive. Their move to Marwell in October did not cure them of their habits, so they went on to Rhenen Zoo, in Holland which had suitable accommodation – thus ended Marwell's brief, and only, encounter with bears.

One feature lacking at Marwell was that there were no natural water features, so one of the early moves after the Zoo had opened was the creation of a pond for the group of Cuban flamingos, that were later to be joined by greater flamingos. The next, the black swan pond near the entrance gate, came shortly after as the result of an accident. John Knowles, the gatekeeper Tom, and Ginger Hazzard who had supplied fruit and vegetables for the Zoo since animals first arrived, were engaged in conversation one morning, when a large explosion, followed by a very high jet of water, heralded a burst in the water main that served the Park. The

View on entering the Park, June 1972, with catering marquee and newly formed black swan pond.

Ralph Thompson draws the Sumatran tiger at the first Society meeting.

water quickly flooded the area that inspired the later construction of the black swan pond – complete with jet fountain! When first filled, this pond was fairly deep and the water crystal clear so it was used by the keepers for after-hours' swimming – an idea not so attractive today now that the pond is rich in green algae and teeming with wildlife.

Despite what must have been enormous pressures to complete the initial zoo layout, John Knowles found time to remember those who had supported his ideas. The Marwell Zoological Society was formed before the opening of the Park, with a nucleus of Marwell supporters from the days of planning difficulties being invited to be honorary Life Members. The first meeting was held on the 3rd November 1972 in the recently completed Treetops. The well respected wildlife artist, Ralph Thompson, was the speaker for this meeting and, in front of the audience drew one of Marwell's Sumatran tigers. The picture was presented to the Society and today it hangs in the offices in the Hall. It was at this meeting too, that John Knowles suggested that the members should take over the operation of the Society with John Seabrook invited to be Chairman and John Adams as Secretary. John Seabrook had to decline because of other commitments, and was replaced by Peggy Jordan who held the chair for the first three years of the Society, while John Adams remained Secretary until appointment as Development Manager in 1992. Peter Hickman, the original Treasurer, continues to hold that post.

Meanwhile Marwell was achieving what it had set out to do, breeding animals, and regular visitors to the Park soon realised that there were always some new youngsters to be seen. All three species of zebra had bred prior to the Park's opening, with further births later in the year, along with nyala, impala, waterbuck, scimitar-horned oryx, blackbuck, European lynx, leopards, Przewalski horses, llama, fallow deer and Cape hunting dogs. Many of these births, such as that of the nyala, were the first ever in the UK, and others were the first that had occured for many decades. It has been the continued success with many of these animals, and the policy of ensuring a good base breeding stock whenever possible, that enabled Marwell-bred animals to be later relocated throughout the world.

Not all of the animals that had been born were reared by their mothers. Marwell received a pair of Cape hunting dogs in June, which had been bred at Whipsnade. Come November it was obvious a birth was imminent and the female appeared to go into the first stages of labour. Her condition was watched over by the veterinary surgeon and, when there seemed to be a problem, the animal was imobilised and examined. It transpired that the position of a pup was preventing a natural birth, so a Caesarian was conducted. Despite difficulties, six pups from the litter of nine were eventually delivered alive, and returned to the Zoo. The mother showed no interest, so bottle-feeding had to be attempted. Hunting dogs had seldom been born in captivity and Marwell had no guidance on their hand-rearing. The deaths

Grévy zebra with foal.

of further pups made it obvious that bottle-rearing was not going to be successful, so an urgent plea was made on the local television to find a domestic dog bitch in milk. The excellent response brought in the services of a mongrel bitch, with the endearing name of Sly, owned by a Mr. and Mrs. Tubb of Winchester. Within hours the three surviving pups were already looking better, and after six weeks were weaned and Sly went back to her home in Winchester.

Although hunting dogs were to breed again at Marwell, they are not an easy species to manage because of their complex social structure. When they first arrived at Marwell they were not considered an endangered species, a situation that has sadly changed. In the future it is hoped to build a specially designed enclosure and keep this species again.

The novelty of such a remarkable collection in Hampshire drew a lot of curious visitors, despite the adverse weather, with over 115,000 coming through the gates in the first four months, which excludes those who returned with free passes. The expectations of the public had, perhaps, been underestimated, as even today Marwell encounters people who visited when the Park first opened, but have not been since. 'We will come back when it is finished' they used to say, but a zoo is never 'finished', it is a living organism, forever evolving and changing.

Scimitar-horned oryx.

Eartha Kitt meets Tiggy in 1973.

CHAPTER FOUR

THE EARLY YEARS

1973 was the year that Britain entered the European Community and, of greater impact to Marwell, was the year that VAT was introduced. The fact that Marwell had dropped its admission price for early visitors, then charged the intended rate and now charged VAT on that rate, made it look like charges were escalating. The fact that the increase was due to the new tax was of no consolation to the visitor who was already price sensitive, and there is no doubt that this, coupled with the changes in Britain's economic climate, had an adverse effect on Marwell's early development. However, there were fundamental needs for Marwell which were not going to be overlooked, so Marwell's committment to education took a step forward by conversion of the old chapel in Marwell Hall into a lecture hall. The Park offered educational facilities, with guided tours for groups even before the Zoo opened to the public, and the first educational pack for school visitors was produced in early June 1972. Martin Banks became Education Officer and conducted these facilities until he left a few years later, eventually to work with Anglian Television's successful *Survival* team.

This year witnessed some milestones, the most famous being the birth and rearing of 'Miko', the tiger cub. To breed these magnificent cats was a prime wish of John Knowles. Boris and Lena never bred, probably because they had been hand-reared, so it was Nimana, one of the Leipzig females, who brought the first tiger cubs to Marwell. She had three cubs in the small hours of the cold, wet, morning of the 1st May. It is not uncommon for big cats to fail to look after their first litter, and Nimana was no exception, although she became an exemplary mother with later litters. She broke into her outside enclosure and scattered her cubs. Two were found dead, but the third, presumed to be the last born, was still alive, and Nimana readily dropped the little bundle when encouraged to return to her den. This male cub was warmed back to life in the Aga of the kitchen, and was then patiently hand-reared by John and Margaret Knowles. Despite the official name of Miko, he was better known as Tiggy, and won the hearts of all who encountered him.

On most days he was brought into the offices until his playfulness and size made it necessary for him to be moved into the new Children's Zoo. It was known to be important not to humanise the animal too much or else his future breeding potential could be lost. An early introduction to a lion cub from Windsor was not successful, so Lara, a female Siberian tiger cub born at Rotterdam Zoo, was obtained in September. Tiggy grew to be a magnificent animal and sired a number of cubs in later years. He died in 1992, and had thus reached a good age for a tiger.

Tiggy was not to be the only cub that needed a surrogate mother. At the end of October, two cubs were born to a leopardess who had previously been a good mother. However, this time she had little or no milk, so the cubs were removed for hand-rearing by the wife of the carnivore keeper, Jeff Webb. One did not thrive for more than a few hours, leaving a single cub, later to be called Cheeko. A week later a single cub was born to a jaguar that was considered unlikely to look after it, so he was also removed. Although days younger, Phoenix, as he was to be called, was the more advanced animal from the start. As the Webb's had a young baby, two cats and a ten-month old alsatian puppy, their household became more lively as the cubs grew! Like Tiggy they eventually moved into the Children's Zoo before graduating to the big cats' cages. The difference between the two species was quite marked throughout their upbringing, with Phoenix quickly becoming a 'wild' animal, while Cheeko remaining docile all his life.

Christine Webb feeding the jaguar cub.

John Knowles with Cleo.

A significant birth was a calf to Cleo, a scimitar-horned oryx, as this was the first second-generation birth of the species at Marwell. To explain the importance of this birth means going back to the start of the story of one of the most important groups of animals in the Zoo. Scimitar-horned oryx are the pride of Marwell and represent well the work that the Park has achieved with desert antelope. The initial group of oryx all came from the Dutch animal dealer, Van den Brink, some of them being wild-caught and others being their progeny. They were imported into quarantine in Salford, then went to the Belle Vue Zoo, Manchester. After ten months there, they were shipped down to Marwell to arrive in November 1971. At that time there were estimated to be some 10,000 surviving in Mali, Niger and Chad, and they had already become extinct in Egypt in the last century, and in Morocco, Algeria; and more recently, Libya, Sudan and Tunisia. The severe poverty in many of the lands around the Sahara, and the strife caused by civil wars, makes the chances of conservation in the wild impractical, and it is the larger mammals that are the first to suffer. In less than the number of years that Marwell has been open, the scimitar-horned oryx has been almost certainly exterminated in its last strongholds. When the oryx arrived for Marwell they were the first specimens to be seen in Britain since 1912, and they were the first to breed, with three being born while in quarantine in Manchester.

Gemsbok with calf.

Because John Knowles foresaw the plight of these animals and realised that building up viable breeding groups in captivity could be the key to survival of many ungulates, the scimitar-horned oryx was chosen to become Marwell's emblem. The oryx started breeding soon after arrival – five in 1971 and five the year after. Cleo had been born while in quarantine in Manchester and had been hand-reared, so it was far from certain if she would breed, or make a good mother. A couple of days after the first anniversary of the opening of the Park she produced a male calf which looked most odd, as it had a disproportionally large head. However, the concerns were unfounded as Cleo was a good mother and the calf grew to a normal adult. Cleo surprised Marwell at a later birth when she produced twins, although neither survived. For most ungulates, a single youngster is normal, and twins are very rare, although twin births of gemsbok and onager have also occured at Marwell. Their chances of survival in the wild are even less than in captivity and this is probably the main reason why the events have been so seldom recorded.

The Przewalski horse is another key species. Now extinct in the wild, this was not known at the time of Marwell's opening. Their survival has been achieved by the continued captive breeding from a stock of wild-caught Przewalski horses that had been imported by the German wild animal dealer, Carl Hagenbeck, in the early 1900s, with the addition of a single wild female captured in 1947. Przewalskis are the only surviving wild horses; the so-called 'brummies' of Australia, and the mustangs of America, are feral domesticated animals. It was these animals that had captured the imagination of John Knowles when he visited the Catskill Game Park in the 1960s, and they were the first animals to arrive in England for Marwell in late 1969 and early 1970. The original group comprised five females from Prague, a pair from the United States of America, and a mare – in foal – who arrived in June 1972 from Rotterdam.

The Prague group of Przewalski horses was the most important in the world. The Dubcek uprising in Czechoslovakia at the time created a political uncertainty and this may have been a factor why Prague saw the wisdom in distributing part of its valuable herd. That John Knowles managed to acquire five mares from Prague shows how seriously international collections were taking his plans for Marwell, and that they had faith in him to succeed.

The male, Basil, was also an important animal, and his breeding prowess was crucial to Marwell's success with the species. Although he had been bred at the Catskill Game Farm, he had not been kept there for many years. Because surplus stallions cannot be kept together in the proximity of females without creating problems, Basil had been sent to a private ranch in Kentucky where he had been kept on his own for a number of years. He had been offered for sale by an animal dealer, Fred Zeehandler, at the quite appreciable sum of $2,000. Basil was certainly a good looking animal, but John Knowles was concerned that the stallion's long period of isolation from his own kind may have had an adverse affect. He cabled Zeehandler to ask 'is this animal a guaranteed breeder?' to which John Knowles received the reply, 'my name is Zeehandler, not God!' Basil duly

Tarpan – social grooming.

arrived, and it was with some trepidation that the horses were first mixed in their paddock in May 1971. Basil behaved just as he would have done in the wild and, after a bit of chasing around by the females, he took command of 'his' herd. When the local hunt broke into the Zoo in 1976, Basil rounded up the herd so that all the females stood in a circle, heads facing outwards, defending their foals, while Basil raced around the circle attacking the intruding hounds. Such a disturbance was a major threat to the horses, and all the mares subsequently aborted. Consequent agreement with the hunt has assured that they are prohibited from the farmland surrounding the Zoo, so such a tragedy should never reoccur.

Marwell has had considerably more than one hundred successful births of Przewalski horses. For a time the Park kept two herds, but the international breeding of this species now means that Marwell does not need to be so productive, and controlled breeding is now being planned. In 1970 there were about 180 Przewalski horses in the world; today there are over 1,000, an improvement that reflects the international co-operation between the zoos. The aim is to introduce a herd of the horses back into the wild, and negotiations have been under way for a number of years, during which time John Knowles has twice visited Mongolia. Such introductions are not only very costly but need careful planning to ensure success.

A unique exhibit at Marwell in the early years were the tarpan. The tarpan was the wild horse of Europe, thought to have become extinct as late as the 1880s, leaving the Przewalski as the only surviving wild horse. The tarpan, however, had been cross-bred with domestic horses in the historic past. During the inter-war years, attempts were made both in Poland and Germany to independently 'recreate' the tarpan by breeding out the domestic horse characteristics. This they did to a remarkable degree, with the resulting animals resembling the original mousy-grey coloured adults, and the foals being the juvenile colour of yellow. Tarpan at Marwell were from both German

European bison.

and Polish stock and they were bred, but it was decided not to continue with this interesting but recreated animal, as space was needed for endangered species.

Appropriately, in an enclosure facing the tarpan, the European bison were kept. These bison had shared the same habitat – the Bialowieza Forest – which had been the last refuge of the tarpan, until it, too, had become extinct in the wild about the time the First World War ended. The European bison has survived through the breeding of the few that remained in captivity, which eventually led to its release back into the Bialowieza Forest. Its increase in numbers caused Marwell to decide to later replace the bison with sitatunga antelope.

The wild asses of the world have also suffered badly by the hands of man, and all of the remaining races are listed as endangered species. Originally Marwell had a trio each of Turkmenian kulan and Persian onager, two very similar looking animals which some authorities today do not consider as different sub-species. Their similarity was such that one of the 'onager' was later identified as a kulan! This left the park with only a pair of onager and, as the kulan started breeding, it made sense to concentrate with the kulan only. Plans are to expand involvement with wild asses, though with the addition of Somali wild ass in 1993.

Completing the equines at Marwell were three species of zebra, Chapman's, Grévy

Kulan.

and Hartmann's mountain. The mountain zebras were the rarest of the three, and proved to be the most difficult to manage as, unlike the other species, they are quite unsociable and it took some years for the Park to build up a compatible group, which is now the second-largest captive herd in the world. The Chapman's zebra is a race of the common zebra and, while quite plentiful, made Marwell one of the few places to exhibit all three species. The Grévy is the largest of the zebras. They were relatively common in the wild at the time the Zoo was opened, with an estimated population of over 30,000, but in a relatively small range of Ethiopia and northern Kenya. The initial group of nine Grévy zebra at Marwell was a wise investment by John Knowles, as the wild population has already fallen to less than 10,000.

The aims of the Park and the nature of the beasts that it concentrated on, unfortunately made close contact by the public neither desireable nor safe. However it was recognised that visitors, especially the younger ones, appreciated the opportunity, so it was for that reason a Children's Zoo was opened in 1973, which was on the site of the present gazelle house and tamarin islands. In addition to domesticated species such as Queen Victoria cream ponies, pot-bellied pigs, dwarf goats and donkeys, the Children's Zoo also accommodated some small exotic mammals, such as coatis, and a number of species of bird. Amongst these were cheer pheasants, a rare species whose conservation programme Marwell was later to get involved with. Under the control of the World Pheasant Association, eggs laid in Britain were flown out to their native Pakistan and northern India where they were hatched under broody bantams and eventually released.

By the end of 1973, Britain was sliding into the worst recession for many years, with wage freezes, threats of petrol rationing and

The original Children's Zoo, now the site of the gazelle house.

Young Chapman's zebra.

'three-day' working weeks. By the end of 1974 inflation stood at 26% and VAT was increased. None of this was conducive to keeping Marwell operating and it was vital that every effort was made to keep up attendances, for the breeding programmes were rapidly increasing the number of mouths to feed, and there was always the wish to take more species on board.

Despite the message that Marwell was different, and despite the clear statement that Marwell's prime aim was to breed endangered species, it was obvious from day one that a sector of the public were so conditioned to the 'picture-book' image of a zoo that they could not consider Marwell as a 'proper' zoo unless it had lions, monkeys and elephants. The fact that the Park kept so many unusual animals that were 'new' to most visitors did not seem to impress and, in hindsight, it was expecting a lot from the public to suddenly become excited in encountering one herd of ungulates after another. Marwell had, however, always kept a number of common species to help balance the collection. Without llamas, guanaco, wallabies and emu, the American and Australasian areas would have been very sparse in the early days, and there were benefits to be learnt from the keeping of these animals that could be applied to their rarer relatives in the future.

The lack of elephants will probably always remain a disappointment for some visitors, but Marwell would not concede to keeping these magnificent animals unless it was able to ensure ample facilities to manage a natural social group and be convinced that, in doing so, there was adequate ethical justification. Perhaps in the future, other zoos may create a surplus of captive-bred elephants, and there will be conservation needs to maintain them in captivity – then that may be the time when John Knowles achieves his dream of being an elephant keeper!

Sulawesi macaque.

Lions and monkeys were different. When Marwell opened, the only chance would have been to obtain African lions, an animal fortunately both common in the wild and kept in abundance in captivity. It was some years later that Marwell acquired the very rare Asiatic lions, and their arrival is told later. John Knowles was not keen to obtain primates, and it was with some reluctance that it was agreed to obtain a pair of Patas monkeys in 1974, partly in order to satisfy the visitors' wishes and to explore the keeping of what was, for Marwell, an entirely new group of animals. He had been encouraged by the new Curator, Peter Bircher, who started at Marwell in the summer of the previous year after working at the Zoological Society of London. As fate would have it, the dealer was unable to supply the promised Patas monkeys and instead, a pair of Celebes apes (now called Sulawesi macaques to meet political and taxomic correctness!) were obtained. These jet black, tailess, monkeys from the swampy forests of this Indonesian island may not be the most beautiful of the monkeys, but they captured the interest of those who cared for them – and that of the visitors. Their success started what was to become an important collection of primates.

New arrivals kept Marwell in the news. The first giraffe birth occured in May 1974 to Dribbles. A rare occurance in the zoo world was the hatching of a Victoria crowned pigeon, a spectacular bird from the forests of New Caledonia. The egg had been incubated under a broody tumbler pigeon and, although the chick lived only ten days, a later squab was reared the following year, making it probably the first in the UK.

Recession or not, animals that had been imported twelve months earlier, and residing in Manchester, had to be moved down to Marwell. They were two groups of African antelope, a male and six female gemsbok from the Kalahari Desert, and two pairs of sable, native to south-east Africa. Later a pair of swamp deer, or barasingha, came from Whipsnade. These, the largest of the Indian deer, were down to around 4,000 individuals in the wild, and 150 in captivity throughout the world.

Other arrivals included a group of six collared peccary from the Jersey Wildlife Preservation Trust, and a group of four Darwin rheas which came via an animal dealer. The collared peccary were not considered a rarity, and were commonly seen in zoological gardens in Britain and abroad. However, while many places had experienced excellent initial breeding results, the breeding coefficient declined annually, and groups of peccary were gradually dying out through old age. The Curator, Peter Bircher, took an interest in the particular plight of the species and became European co-ordinator for their propagation. Subsequent research showed that peccaries have a reluctance to breed with closely related stock, a natural defence against the problems of in-breeding. It was therefore vital that new stock was introduced to each peccary group from time to time to maintain a continuation of births. Introduction of new animals at Marwell, and elsewhere, has resulted in births again.

The captive-bred Darwin rheas were imported as chicks and were the only ones in Britain. As they matured it became clear that there were three cock birds and only one hen. Although they lived for a few years, they were not destined for success as the adult birds developed a problem with their legs caused by untreatable infections. Marwell had developed a particular interest in the ratites, the large flightless birds of which the Darwin rheas were an example, and at this time had representatives from all of their native countries, rheas from South America; cassowary from New Guinea; emu from Australia and ostrich from Africa. The rheas bred well, to the extent that the early hatchings – 112 reared in 1973 – flooded the market and the future breeding was controlled to ensure that birds did not become surplus to requirements. In 1974, the first ostrich was hatched at Marwell in an incubator, and in later years, the first UK natural hatching and rearing was achieved.

Czechoslovakia, in anticipation of their move. To Marwell's surprise, air travel became the most logical way to move the animals, and a Britannia 737 was eventually chartered and stripped out to move the camels in two groups of fourteen. After delayed departure caused by a French air strike, the jet

Off-loading camels from the 737.

The major arrival of animals at Marwell, though, must have been the herd of twenty-nine camels which, with the two already in the Park, brought the grand total to thirty-one beasts! Their story, however, goes back to 1973 when the opportunity arose to import a group of Bactrian camels from Europe. The eventual aim would be to export camels on to Canada to meet the demand for the animals in the United States of America, where, because of quarantine regulations, it was not permissible to import directly. The animals, which are a domesticated species, had originated in Russia, and had been assembled in Prague,

eventually left Luton Airport empty, except for Marwell staff needed to accompany the camels on their return journey. The plane returned safely to Manchester, with its first batch of camels, which were off-loaded, to the interest of the Press and television, ready to be taken to Belle Vue, Manchester, to start their mandatory quarantine. The camels had to leave their travelling crates and be loaded into cattle lorries to take them to Belle Vue, so that the crates could be returned on the waiting 737 for the shipment of the second group of animals. By now, most of the camels were happily used to the travelling and were settled sitting in their crates, so it took some motivation to persuade the beasts that they had to vacate their crates and enter the waiting trucks. Somehow the whole manoeuvre was achieved between the 2.30 p.m. touchdown and the 4.00 p.m. departure of the plane back to Prague. Back in Prague, the zoo staff were found efficiently awaiting the loading of the animals in temperatures of –10°C. This load included two large bulls, whose humps brushed the light fittings in the plane; however, within five minutes of being in the air, all of the camels had settled into a sitting position for an uneventful flight.

Over a year later the herd was moved by road down south to Marwell; the number increased by one because of two births, and one death, while in Manchester. Not too surprisingly, eleven camels were born at Marwell before the eventual redistribution of the animals, leaving the Park with a more manageable-sized herd. Camels, with their reputation for stubborness, spitting and the ability to kick from all four corners, are not the most endearing of animals, and Jon Barzdo, who was their keeper of the time, penned the lines:

'I don't really dote
on camels with a coat
but camels moulting
are pretty revolting.'

To remember Jon Barzdo for his poetry, however, is a disservice, as he was one of the early keeping staff who, while at Marwell, founded the Association of British Wild Animal Keepers, an organisation that has achieved significant advances, not only in the improved management of animals in captivity but also in instigating training courses for the further education of people working in the zoo profession. The EEC is now looking at how similar measures can be introduced to improve the rest of the European zoo community.

The Marwell Zoological Society obtained charity status at the end of 1974, an important development, as it was then able to raise funds to support the work that Marwell was doing. John Knowles had intended from the start that the Zoo would become a charitable trust as soon as it was apparent that the operation was a viable concern. Effectively this meant that the daily operating costs had to be covered by the gate receipts, for the Zoo received no other financial support. In the then current economic situation, the future of the Park was far from secure. The fact that the Society had developed sufficiently to become a registered charity gave some hope for the future and, indeed, the support that the Society was able to give for particular projects at Marwell proved to be a valuable asset through a period of economic gloom.

Previously, a token payment had been made by the Society to the Zoo for the right of admission into the Park. Immediately the Society achieved charity status, John Knowles waived all payments, and ever since every member has been granted free admission to the Zoo in acknowledgement of the Society's support.

The Society promptly launched a fund-raising campaign, initially called 'Operation Snow Leopard', for the simple reason that snow leopards were high on the priority list of species that Marwell wished to become

Snow leopard.

concerned with. The fund was later renamed 'The Ark Fund' to avoid confusion, as it was intended for all manner of projects, and not only those related to snow leopards. Operation Snow Leopard was launched, in grand style, at Marwell Hall on the 30th May 1975, with John Aspinall as guest of honour and, to emphasise the point that the campaign was not only about snow leopards, announced that the first project would be to raise £2,000 to obtain maned wolves. Marwell achieved its fund-raising target in 1975, and the magnificent long-legged, red coated, animals arrived in July – then tragedy struck with the pair dying within ten days of arrival. It says much to the credit of the Society members and their respect for the Park, that they raised money again for maned wolves and obtained a second pair. The result was that Marwell succeeded in breeding these remarkable animals for the first time in the UK in 1983.

The red pandas, which had been scheduled to arrive for the Park's opening, eventually arrived in the spring of 1975. These, the only relation of the better-known but even rarer giant panda, are also distinctive creatures, with bushy tails, rich chestnut-coloured coats and, unusual in mammals, a black belly. The originally intended quarters – a walled enclosure near the wild asses – had, in the meanwhile, been occupied by porcupines and, later, coatis, so a new enclosure was built for them around a tall living oak tree, which was much appreciated by these arboreal animals. Marwell has bred red pandas a number of times, the best remembered youngster being Moggi who was hand-reared by Peter Bircher. As a result of his interest in these animals, Peter Bircher has become joint European co-ordinator for the species. In recent years Marwell has imported and quarantined a number of red pandas which have been distributed to other collections in order to increase the breeding potential.

The antelope species increased with the arrival of a pair of addax in 1975. Addax were to become another significant species for the Park, and later built up to become a strong group of these animals. These animals, from the harsh, dry Sahara Desert are unusual amongst antelope, as they appear to pair-bond, and also have a seasonal coat colour change. The first pair had been quarantined at Edinburgh Zoo and they were eventually returned to Edinburgh some years later as a pair, to start a new group there once the numbers had increased at Marwell.

While the addax may have been unaffected by it, 1976 brought the worst drought to Britain for 240 years. This did little to encourage visitors to the park in the heat of the summer, and the paddocks dried to create an even more naturalistic savannah grassland for many of the African animals.

Perhaps because of the weather, breeding results on the bird section were particularly good, and the tortoises laid eggs for the first time – although success with hatching and rearing tortoises was to come in later years.

New legislation this year put import restrictions on birds so, not before time, virtually no exotic wild birds could be brought into Britain without a licence. The other legislation that year, that was aimed to control some of the less desireable aspects of private exotic animal keeping, was the Dangerous Wild Animals Act. The law had no direct implications for zoos, but it did increase the number of enquiries from individuals wishing to place exotic animals that they could no longer keep.

Red panda, 'Moggi'.

While 1976 had seemed a fairly uneventful year, 1977 was quite the reverse, ending the season with headline coverage of Marwell in newspapers and on television around the world. The most important new species to arrive was undoubtedly the first snow leopard, Vilkku. She was the first stage in the realisation of a long cherished dream by John Knowles to keep this, arguably, most beautiful of all cats. Less than thirty snow leopards had ever been seen in Britain since the first ones arrived at London Zoo at the beginning of the century. John Knowles particularly remembered two that had been shown by the late Sir Bailey Fossett, in Sir Robert Fossett's Circus.

The Marwell Zoological Society had raised the funds needed to import this animal, and later paid to obtain her mate, Pavel, from Seattle, and to provide their accommodation. John Knowles went to Helsinki and met Vilkku, a nine-year-old female who had been bred at that zoo and had since reared her own cubs.

Less well publicised, but to prove important too, was the arrival of a trio of secretary birds. These long-legged birds of prey are unlike any other raptor and, although they are good fliers, spend much of their time hunting prey on the ground. Although not uncommonly kept, these birds had never been bred in captivity. It has been common practice for zoos to clip the wings of these mainly ground-dwelling birds so that they could be kept 'at liberty', but Marwell reasoned that the full use of wings may be critical to the successful mating of these birds, and it was therefore decided to keep them in a covered aviary. This policy proved valuable as later developments would show.

The most famous arrival – and departure – though, proved to be Victor, the giraffe. Victor had been born at Whipsnade Zoo and had been named after Victor Manton, the then curator at Whipsnade. He was brought to Marwell in April to replace the bull giraffe that had died over a year previously, leaving three females, Arabesque, Dribbles and Domino. Quite what happened will never be known, but on the morning of 15th September, Victor was found down on the ground and was unable to get up. Despite the insistence of the subsequent press coverage, there was no evidence that he had fallen while trying to mate.

Giraffes are not only the tallest living animal, but one of the heavier land mammals, with a bull weighing a much as a ton. Their physiology is as remarkable as their anatomy, with a unique system of blood distribution that prevents giddiness when the animal raises its head. When a giraffe lies with its head on the ground, its blood pressure can more than double. As with many large mammals, such as elephants, they are unable to lie on the ground for long because the weight on the rib cage will gradually compress the internal organs. In the wild a giraffe in such a plight would quickly fall prey to predators; in captivity the need was to get the animal back on its feet as quickly as possible.

Victor remained on the ground for six days, despite valiant attempts to lift him. The media attention turned from one of amusement

to one of concern, as the true plight of the animal became fully appreciated. In the words of the *Daily Express* columnist, Jean Rook, 'For six anxious days, our thoughts, our news bulletins, and our prayers have been weighed down by a one-ton fifteen-year-old giraffe. Advice, and tears, have poured into his sick-pen from a nation united, all eyes on the skyline, in their grief.'

The attention of the press had never been anticipated, nor likely to be ever repeated, but the fate of poor Victor had now become international news. Victor became front page news as far away as South America and the Middle East, and Marwell was told that film news reports were shown in every country that had a television service.

Victor died, in the public gaze of the television cameras, with his head on the shoulder of John Knowles, after a valiant fight for life. He had suffered a massive heart attack as a result of the stress imposed by his traumatic situation. A few weeks later at a zoo in Japan, a giraffe managed to repeat the tragedy, but received only passing mention in a few newspapers. Such accidents occur daily in the animal kingdom, yet for some reason

Victor.

the story of Victor touched on the hearts of the world. The memory of Victor, however, lived on, and when the giraffe calf, Victoria was born to Dribbles the following summer there was worldwide media interest again, despite the fact the calf had been conceived, by Victor, long before his fall.

Unsolicited donations and countless letters and goodwill messages arrived for Victor. The donations were used towards the accommodation for the first marmosets and tamarins at Marwell, and the consequent developments with this group of primates gives some consolation from the sad fate of Marwell's most famous animal. The death of Victor heralded the end of the first era of Marwell, for in the following year the Zoo would become a charitable trust.

The second herd of Przewalski horses when kept behind Marwell Hall.

CHAPTER FIVE

THE MARWELL PRESERVATION TRUST – A NEW BEGINNING

In March 1978 the Marwell Preservation Trust Limited was created, and John Knowles transferred the grounds of the Zoological Park and the undeveloped land of the adjacent valley, with the animals, their houses and enclosures, and his former home, Marwell Hall, to the Trust. This generous move brought security for the future of Marwell Zoological Park, and for the continuation of the animal breeding, conservation and educational work in hand. There were just two exceptions to the animals deposited with the Trust: Tiggy, the first Siberian tiger cub that John and Margaret Knowles had saved, and Roo, an orphan wallaby that they had also hand-reared in their home.

Tim Walker was elected as Chairman of the Trust. He was, at that time, also Chairman of the World Wildlife Fund (now known as the World Wide Fund for Nature) and also an enthusiastic breeder of exotic animals at his home, Midway Manor near Bradford-on-Avon. John Knowles and Tim Walker had met by a chance situation. Marwell had sold some blackbuck antelope through an animal dealer and, for practical reasons, had also agreed to deliver the animals direct to the purchaser. Marwell's curator, Peter Bircher, took the animals down to Midway Manor and, on returning to Marwell, suggested to John Knowles that he should contact the Walkers as they had an interest in animals much akin to his own. Thus started a valuable friendship which developed Tim Walker's involvement with wildlife conservation and the expansion of his private animal collection which, at one time, included Grévy zebras, Congo buffalo, waterbuck, alpaca, albino emu and a fine owl collection. It was a tragic blow when, after a short illness, Tim died at the age of forty-six. He was succeeded by the current Chairman, Nick Jonas, in 1988.

Whether it was the legacy of publicity created by Victor, and his subsequent daughter's birth, or the publicity surrounding the creation of the Marwell Preservation Trust, is not known, but 1978 saw the greatest influx of visitors since 1972, with a total attendance of 298,639 paid admissions.

The year saw some notable arrivals too, the rarest being a pair of Asiatic lions, which had been purchased for the then, considerable sum of £6,000 by the Marwell Zoological Society. These lions had been captive-bred in East Berlin, and were later to be joined by the elderly pair from the Jersey Wildlife Preservation Trust, thus making Marwell holder of all of the Asiatic lions in Britain. It had been hoped that the Jersey animals, although not likely to breed themselves, would trigger breeding behaviour between the other pair. It did not, which, with later knowledge, was just as well, as genetic research undertaken in the United States of America discovered that at some time in the past African lions had been crossed with Asiatic animals and therefore much of the captive stock was not pure. This was a serious set back to the conservation of the Asiatic lion, as its numbers in the Gir Forest – its only wild refuge – was under 300, and its future survival may well rest on those in captivity. Marwell has continued to keep the lions, but will not breed from them until pure stock is available.

Asiatic lioness.

The big cat that created greater interest that year, though, was Tunja, a black jaguar, which may have been the first specimen of this colour form ever exhibited in Britain. Although Marwell had no particular intention of concentrating on keeping unusual colour forms of big cats, it already had a black leopard, and the opportunity to compare the two was an unusual one. This year too, the first pair of Arabian gazelle arrived, from Chester Zoo. These petite animals were the start of what would become a thriving group of these rare gazelles.

Young Arabian gazelle.

The first of two National Wildlife Fairs was held in 1979; they were the brainchild of Marwell, to bring together animal organisations and conservation bodies from throughout the UK, with activities and displays linking the countryside, farming and the community – a mix that met with great interest. The Fairs were under the patronage of HRH The Duke of Edinburgh. At the first Fair, Sir Peter Scott, who was in Peking at the time, cabled David Shepherd, the wildlife artist, to announce that the Chinese were to join the World Wildlife Fund and would sign the Washington Convention on the International Trade in Endangered Species. Sir Peter Scott was present at the second Fair; amongst the many celebrities who attended the Fairs were: David Attenborough, David Bellamy, Johnny Morris, Anthony Smith, Leslie Crowther, Tony Soper, Pete Murray, Dinah Sheridan and her daughter Jenny Handley, and the Spinners. It was with regret that the second Fair turned out to be the last. No sponsors could be found and Marwell, which had financially backed the whole undertaking, could not take the risk of losing money should future events not pay – it would only have taken a rainy day to have destroyed all that had been achieved.

Tragedy did strike with a series of sudden deaths, that still remain a mystery. Within the space of four days, four cats were lost; Vilkku the snow leopard, a cheetah, a Northern lynx and a serval. Each death was in a different part of the Park, and other cats kept in the same areas were not affected. The most likely theory was poisoning, either accidently with contaminated meat, or intentionally by a third party, but this was never proven.

Notable births that year were the first black jaguar cubs, and the first Congo buffalo ever bred in Britain. The buffalo had arrived in the spring and were probably the first living examples to be seen in Britain. Although they are considered by some authorities to be the same species as the Cape buffalo, they are quite different in being not only much smaller, but having red coats, long-haired ears and distinctive small horns.

Towards the end of 1980 a young male black rhinoceros, Kes, arrived from Regent's Park,

Young black jaguar, bred in 1985.

and a female, Katie, bred at Whipsnade, arrived in the following June. All rhinoceros species are severely threatened animals, and their chances of survival into the next millennium is very bleak indeed. The black rhinoceros, the smaller of the two African species, has declined dramatically in the wild due to escalation of illegal hunting, encouraged by the ridiculously high prices paid for its horn. Because black rhinoceroses tend to be solitary animals, few zoos have the resources to keep more than a pair, and the addition of these animals to Marwell was planned as a further refuge for the captive stock. The rhino, whose quarters were paid for by the Society, grew well and appeared to be in excellent condition. Six years later, Kes fell into a period of poor health, showing symptoms that had been seen in other black rhinos. He underwent a programme of veterinary treatment, with high hopes of saving his life, but that was not to be. Katie had, in the meantime remained quite normal, so it was completely unexpected when she was found to have died overnight only three weeks later. The subsequent post-mortem proved that the male had fallen victim to a form of oedema, caused through the apparent difficulty that black rhinos have with Vitamin E assimilation. The proximity of the death of the female was entirely co-incidental, as this was found to have been caused by a heart defect.

Black rhinoceros, 'Kes'.

Marwell now has two pairs of white rhinos. Adult white rhinos can obtain a shoulder height of 1·85 metres (six feet) and a weight of 3,600 kg (3½ tons) which is appreciably more than the black rhinoceros. It soon became apparent that the animals were rapidly out-growing their house when they rested their front legs on the walls and started lifting the roof with their horns! So in the summer of 1992 the building was extended in size to provide pens suitable for breeding cows and to facilitate indoor public viewing, and the roof was raised by a metre in height. The rhinos are mixed in

White rhinoceros.

Off-loading the white rhinoceros by crane.

the paddock with a herd of greater kudu. Surprisingly, these antelope are the dominant animals, and the male kudu has no qualms in chasing off the rhino when he wishes.

In June 1981, the first snow leopard cub was born to Vanda, the father being Pavel. When Pavel had arrived from America he showed all the signs of stereotyped behaviour, which greatly concerned the staff at Marwell. He was also obviously stressed by his move and refused to eat for many days. Slowly he settled in and he became a transformed animal, losing his stereotypic movements and developing a wonderful temperament. Like the Siberian tigers, the snow leopards are usually well-tempered animals with strong personalities. There is evidence that they pair-bond, and certainly dislike changes in their life-style. Snow leopards have prospered well in captivity during the last twelve years, with the result that they are now kept and bred in an increasing number of zoos in Britain. The fact remains, though, that the status of the snow leopard in the wild has not improved, so the need to maintain the situation in captivity is important.

Snow leopard. Vanda with the first cub to be born at Marwell, Pavan.

Roan antelope.

The tenth anniversary year of the opening of the Park was celebrated in style, with a special weekend of entertainment, to which the Variety Club of Great Britain brought 300 under-privileged children.

Although the Park had catered for educational visits from the start, there was a long-standing commitment to build on this as soon as resources became available. In this anniversary year an agreement was reached with the Manpower Services Commission and the Marwell Preservation Trust to establish an Education Centre and Services based in Marwell Hall so, at the start of the year, a Community Enterprise Project employed two teachers and a graphic artist. The Hall's former chapel was converted into an Education Centre, which was formally opened by the Chairman of the Hampshire County Council Education Committee.

Because the scheme was funded by the Manpower Services Commission, those employed under the scheme could only work for twelve months. One of the teachers, Clare Sulston, was allowed to continue through the second year, as Senior Education Officer, in order to ensure the continuity necessary for the educational programmes. Towards the end of 1984 the value of the Education Centre was recognised by the Hampshire County Council, and a formal association was made with the Hampshire Education Authority in 1985 which enabled Clare Sulston to be permanently appointed as Head of Department and for the facilities of the Centre to be extended.

When the Manpower Services Commission scheme ceased in 1988 there was great concern that the use of the Education Centre would have to be drastically reduced, but the Hampshire Education Authority agreed to extend their input and thus ensure that all schools in the region would benefit. In addition to catering for some 30,000 school children a year, the Centre provides services for the Zoo visitor including guided tours, touch tables and animal handling demonstrations; operates meetings for junior members of the Society and stages exhibitions, talks and courses away from Marwell. The Education Centre also produces most of the graphics, information and identification signs that are used around the Park, with much of the original artwork produced by the resident artist, Paddy Weeks.

The Park continued to introduce rare species; 1982 saw the arrival of Persian leopards, Malayan tapirs and roan antelope, while the following year brought pygmy hippopotamus, sitatunga, Arabian oryx and several primates.

Young Persian leopard in an oak tree.

The Persian leopards were the rarest animals in the Zoo. Extinct in the wild, the survival of this distinctive race was dependent upon the sixty animals registered in captivity at the time. Marwell has since had four litters of cubs, and the world population has crept up to 150.

Arabian oryx.

The story of the saving of the Arabian oryx from extermination is a remarkable one. From a stock of less than thirty individuals that were assembled in captivity in 1963, the world herd had grown to over 600. It was appropriate that Marwell should receive this relative of the scimitar-horned oryx as the web of collections keeping this species expanded. The arrival of the Arabian oryx, along with the roan antelope, meant that Marwell now kept the most comprehensive collection of this group of antelope, the hippotraginae; the only omissions being the besia and the fringe-eared oryx, which are both sub-species of the gemsbok.

Pygmy hippopotamus.

The Malayan tapirs and pygmy hippo, were scheduled to reside in a new house, to also accommodate the Park's Brazilian tapirs. The building was more permanent in design than most of the others around the Zoo as it had to incorporate a deep pool for each of the three species, as well as provide a warm environment. This semi-aquatic mammal house was officially opened by HRH The Duchess of Kent on the 3rd October 1984, and was welcomed by Park staff and visitors alike as one of the few warm spots in the Zoo throughout the year!

Malayan tapirs and baby.

HRH The Duchess of Kent greeting trustee Jane Cole at the opening of the semi-aquatic mammal house.

One of the great rarities in zoos is the okapi. This sole relation of the giraffe was not discovered until 1901. Its population in the Congo is not known, but the political instability of that part of Africa means that there is little chance of further okapi becoming available from the wild in the foreseeable future, so those in captivity are particularly treasured. Marwell's first okapi was Papyrus who arrived in 1984; he was not a young animal and had come with a history of health problems, but he was to become a much-loved animal who lived until 1990 at the age of fifteen and a half years. In his second season at Marwell he had the company of Harry, a baby giraffe that was being hand-reared; Harry is now the breeding bull of the giraffe group, and the present pair of okapi are now kept in the giraffe house.

On the 13th September 1984, Marwell succeeded in breeding cheetah. Cheetah have long been an enigma to the zoo world because, although these cats were easy to keep and settled well in captivity, often becoming very tame, they were difficult to breed; the first birth being in 1956. Whipsnade Zoo had been a pioneer in the breeding of cheetah regularly, when they determined that familiarity and domesticity were two factors not conducive to success. It was somewhat appropriate that Victor Manton, curator of Whipsnade Park, was at Marwell on the day that the first cheetah birth occured. All five of these

First litter of cheetah cubs, born to Dusky.

original cubs survived, and Marwell has bred these cats a number of times since, including one, Suzie, who was hand-reared by the cat keepers, Phil Hindmarsh and Shaun Belcher.

Blue duiker, a Chilean pudu, siamang gibbons and golden lion tamarins were other notable arrivals that year. The blue duiker were to share the dubious distinction, along with the orange-rumped agoutis that arrived in later years, of being a species kept and bred at

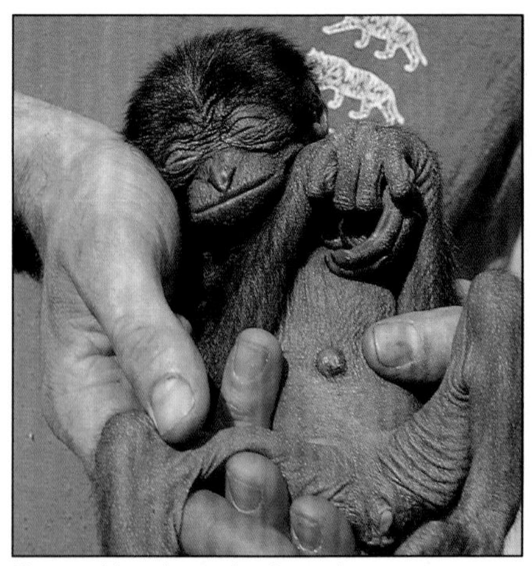

Siamang gibbon that was hand-reared.

Marwell but not put on public exhibition. The golden lion tamarins are spectacularly coloured primates from the Brazilian rain forests. They have suffered severe pressure from man, particularly from the past pet and laboratory trade. They became so rare that in the 1970s the elderly single male – which was an ex-laboratory animal – at London Zoo was considered likely to be the last of the species to be seen in Britain.

The Smithsonian Institution, at the National Zoological Park in Washington DC holds the Stud Book for this species, and they co-ordinate the breeding programme for these monkeys internationally. As the captive populations grew, more collections were given the opportunity to keep them, and Marwell initially received a male from Los Angeles and a female from London. Since then a number have been reared in the Zoo and five of these have been returned as part of a reintroduction programme to the wild. One lesson learnt from the early reintroductions was that the captive-bred animals, used to fixed branches and perches in captivity, found it hard to adjust to the moving plantlife in the forest's canopy, so now, thin twigs and unsupported branches feature in their Zoo quarters.

Although 1984 ended as being the most productive year so far, with 159 mammalian births, the harsh reality remained that the economic climate was not favourable, and Marwell had to continue working hard to achieve progress.

Golden lion tamarin.

Blue duiker, which bred, but not on exhibition.

One of the aims of the Federation of Zoological Gardens of Great Britain and Ireland was to raise the standards of zoological gardens and to introduce a system of control to ensure that these standards were maintained. Marwell was on the Council of the Federation, and John Knowles was also Chairman of the Conservation and Animal Management Committee at the time that the Federation instigated the Zoo Licencing Act that became law in 1984. From then on, all collections that charged admission to the public would require a licence, and would be regularly inspected to ensure that standards were maintained. Failure to attend to the matters raised from inspections could mean loss of the licence and closure of the Zoo. This improvement, which would entail costs to all of the places concerned, illustrates how the zoo community had united in recent years. Fewer and fewer animals were sold, as it was now common practice to exchange animals between collections to the benefit of the species rather than the benefit of the zoological garden. When Marwell had started with Hartmann mountain zebras, it reached agreement with Whipsnade Park that the animals in the two collections would be shared in order to maximise the breeding potential. The move had been advanced considerably when an agreement was reached to merge ownership of twenty-eight species of ungulate kept at Marwell and the Zoological Society of London's two zoos at Regent's Park and Whipsnade.

Scimitar-horned oryx from Marwell back in Tunisia, Bou-Hedma.

Just sometimes, animals come to Marwell for non-breeding purposes. In 1985 two reindeer arrived, from Whipsnade, to help the Zoo, and Santa Claus, with a pre-Christmas extravaganza at Marwell Hall, called 'Winter Wonderland'. Marwell's fairly humble attempt to provide an attraction for winter visitors, and the community of young-at-hearts, exceeded expectations by drawing over 3,300 people on two weekends. Perhaps it was the magic of the reindeer, but the event has grown and grown, so it would now be impossible not to have the Winter Wonderland.

Other animals learn where they are safe. In the early days of the Zoo, the Hampshire Wildfowlers' Association donated six greylag geese. Although the original birds had their wings pinioned, their offspring did not, and had free flight of the countryside but came back to the Zoo to feed and breed. Their numbers did not increase, however, until a fox-proof fence was erected around the flamingos; the geese seemed to instantly appreciate that the fence created a safe haven, and from then on nested annually amongst the flamingos. Most visitors are quite surprised when they see what they thought was a flock of captive birds suddenly fly off.

The story of Marwell's herd of scimitar-horned oryx developed when the first stage of a reintroduction programme for the animals occured in 1985. Preparation of a 2,400 hectare area suitable for the project had commenced eight years previously in Tunisia's Bou-Hedma reserve. By enclosing this large area to prevent the activities of humans and, especially, the depradation of goats, the vegetation, thus protected, recovered dramatically. Dr. Brian Bertram, then the Curator of Mammals at London Zoo, had visited the area and confirmed that it was ready for the first animals to be returned since their extinction in 1935. Thus ten animals from the joint Marwell, Whipsnade and Edinburgh herd left Marwell on the 9th December, by air to Tunis and then by road to the release site. On the fringe of the Sahara, rain caused the most unexpected, but only, problem when one of the vehicles got bogged down in the resulting mud. However, the animals arrived safely without further mishap and were settled into their new quarters. The plan for the release programme was that the original group would be kept in facilities similar to those to which they had been accustomed to in order to acclimatise before being given access to a larger, but fenced, area to adjust to finding food and living in the new terrain. The youngsters born would eventually be fully released.

The following year saw a further animal reintroduction, but this time for Père David's deer. The peculiar saga of this distinctive deer has been related many times; in summary, its wild origin is unknown, but it had survived within the huge walled estate of the Imperial Hunting Park, near Peking. As a result of the Boxer uprising the herd was exterminated, thus leaving the future for the species dependent on the breeding from the few animals that had previously been exported from China. Although Marwell had no significant role in this project, the two animals at Marwell were returned to Whipsnade to join the group that were shipped to China. The World Wildlife Fund in Switzerland had reached an agreement with the Chinese that the deer could be returned to their native land, and a reserve had been created for them on the coast of the Yellow Sea.

Also in 1986, a pair of vicuna were received at Marwell. These wild relations of the llama had been severely persecuted by man in the past because their wool is the finest of any animal in the world. The animals were slaughtered in their thousands for the wool, and their consequent decline only added to its value. Conservation in the wild, and a ban on the international trade in the fleece, has allowed the vicuna to recover. Marwell welcomed the opportunity to keep, and later breed, the only rare South American cameloid, having kept both guanaco and the domesticated llama previously.

Llamas were not the only domesticated animals that have been kept in the Park. Largest was to be a Poitou donkey, a rare breed from the Poitou region of France that can stand up to fifteen hands high (five foot); he was then the only example in Britain.

In that year, 1986, the Marwell Preservation Trust looked hard into the future of the Zoo, and produced a fifteen-year outline development plan which was published with the Trust's Annual Report in the spring of 1987.

Young male Poitou donkey.

HRH The Princess Royal speaking to John Knowles and head keeper, Phil Hindmarsh, with tiger cub.

CHAPTER SIX

PLANS FOR THE FUTURE

1987 saw many more milestones along Marwell's short history, and included the first stage of Marwell's track railway, the installation of some of the features from the Development Plan, the birth of the first scimitar-horned oryx back in its native Tunisia, and the first visit to the park by HRH The Princess Royal.

One of the fundamental factors in replanning the Zoo was the introduction of a fifteen inch gauge railway. There was no doubt that cars in the Park were not welcome by most of our visitors, although it was also recognised that the use of cars was appreciated during periods of inclement weather, and for the benefit of those who find the two-and-a-quarter mile walk around the Zoo difficult. By phasing in alternative transport, Marwell could control the number of cars in the Zoo and, at peak times only allow entry for disabled visitors' vehicles. Initially a single track was installed, starting from the gift shop and running alongside the paddocks, past the jaguar enclosure and then crossing the south section valley on a raised embankment and east, past the rhinos to a terminus near the snow leopards. This gave the opportunity to refence the paddocks to give unobstructed views of the animals, and the moating of the kudu paddock meant that the white rhinoceroses could benefit from sharing the enclosure. The Marwell Zoological Society contributed towards this work by financing a large walk-through area in the adjacent woodland for the wallabies. A new catering facility, toilet block, relandscaped ponds in front of the gazelle house, barless enclosures for meerkats and other small carnivores, an adventure playground for children and a fenceless compound for camels were all also achieved in the first two years of the plan.

The other fundamental move that gave the Trust the security to progress much of this work, was the decision to sell a site on the edge of the Zoo's car park for the erection of a hotel. 'Resort Hotels' was a relatively new and expanding company, already with a distinctive chain of hotels in the south-east of Britain. The design of the new hotel was a unique solution to suit the woodland setting and to blend with the character of the Zoological Park. Only the timber-faced reception and amenity building, with the trees towering behind, can be seen on approaching the Hotel. The bedrooms are in buildings grouped in the woodland behind, and are reached through covered walkways. The colonial style suited not only the English setting, but reflected also the exotic countries associated with the Zoo. Apart from the advantages of having the Hotel amenities close to the Zoo, the main benefit to the Trust was that the capital from the sale would buffer the Trust through the annual problems

Marwell's wonderful railway passing the white rhinoceros paddock.

of cash-flow and the resultant Bank charges, that are inevitable with a business that is governed by seasonal trade. The Marwell Resort Hotel was officially opened in 1990, and has since expanded by building additional conference facilities.

The track train proved immensely popular in its first year, and the intended extension of the track was brought forward. The gradients around the Park made it impractical to take the train along the route originally suggested. The solution was to extend the track as far as the site would allow and to create a loop at both ends to ease the operation of the railway, and then to introduce a road train to serve the remaining part of the Zoo. It was decided to make the road train a free service to visitors, but to continue to charge for the track railway. Qualms that this would reduce the number of people using the track railway proved to be unfounded.

Marwell has an earlier link with railways. The steam locomotives of the Great Western Railway had a 'Hall' series, and all of the engines were named after buildings in the vicinity of the Great Western area. One, number 5946, which has long vanished, was named 'Marwell Hall'. Its name-plate was auctioned in 1988, and probably now resides with a private collector of railway memorabilia.

The extension of the railway created the opportunity to form a water moat around an island for primates at the east end of the track. Initially this was inhabited by a small group of squirrel monkeys, with summertime accommodation on the island. More recently, the Marwell Zoological Society has paid for the island to be modified. New housing was built alongside the moat, with a bridge crossing from it to the island, so that the group of Sulawesi macaques could be reaccommodated in 1992.

The favourable impact of the moated paddocks along the South Road resulted in the creation of dry ditches to replace the existing fences to the large paddocks along Jubilee Avenue, so named because of the avenue of twenty-five trees planted there for the Queen's Silver Jubilee celebrations in 1977.

All these developments stretched the Trust's resources to the limits, so further major change would be dependent upon outside funding. The Marwell Zoological Society undertook the proposed facilities for lemurs and launched its largest fund-raising campaign to date, Lemur Lifeline. The campaign was to take longer than originally envisaged for the simple reason that changes to the design, as the project developed, would significantly increase the cost. The site selected was the old walled kitchen garden of the Hall, an enclosed area behind the stable yard which has not been previously open to the public. The old hand-made brick walls of the garden created a sun-trap which would be ideal for the warmth-loving lemurs, and the opening up of the area would ensure repair to the walls where they had been neglected in the past, making a feature of their architecture. The animal housing would, therefore, be constructed externally to the kitchen garden, with access for the animals into outdoor enclosures within the walled gardens. The public would be led through the area within a glass-walled, covered, walkway and, by the routing of these it proved possible to walk though the exhibit without any steps, despite the quite appreciable fall of land. The building was designed to accommodate four species of lemur.

Red-ruffed lemur.

Coquerel's dwarf lemur.

Red-ruffed, and black-and-white-ruffed, lemurs were the first to arrive for quarantine in 1991, and the following year saw the addition of a troupe of ring-tailed lemurs. The most exciting inmates, though, were two pairs of rare Coquerel's dwarf lemurs. These nocturnal animals had been bred at the Duke Primate Centre, in America, and their arrival made Marwell only the seventh collection in the world with the species outside their native Madagascar. In 1992 both females produced and reared young.

Back to 1987. On the 23rd June the Home Farm Trust, the charity that provides homes and care for people with a mental handicap, celebrated their twenty-fifth anniversary at Marwell Zoological Park, and the Park was honoured by a visit from their patron, HRH The Princess Royal. The Princess agreed to officially inaugurate the track railway, and the engine was named *Princess Anne*. The engine was not alone in being named after the Princess, as the giraffe calf born to Dribbles that year had also been named Anne, following the Park's tradition of naming giraffes born after members of royalty.

The elements had their affect on the Park. In March, gales caused the old cedar of Lebanon on the back lawn to crack in half, and while the lower portion has managed to survive, it has destroyed the beauty of a tree that has watched over events at Marwell for three hundred years. The famous storm of 15th October caused much havoc, felling many trees and limbs. The roof of the camel house was lifted off and the pheasantry and muntjac area was a scene of devastation. However, the only losses were four ring-necked parakeets that disappeared never to be seen again. The resultant power cuts were as big a cause for concern, as only part of the Park had the benefit of a generator for stand-by electricity. A number of the smaller primates were moved to the Curator's kitchen to ensure adequate heat.

The day after the storm, the Zoo, normally open every day of the year except Christmas Day, closed its gates for the safety of the public while the clearing-up operation went on.

An adult secretary bird.

The secretary birds had matured. Although in many birds the differentiation of the sexes is very easy because of the adult plumage, with other species such as penguins, many parrots and some birds of prey, it is impossible without clinical examination. A fairly straightforward system to clinically sex birds had now been devised, and the technique, when used at Marwell had enabled the correct pairing of a number of birds, and the Park now knew it had a true pair of secretary birds. One egg was laid in 1987, and five in 1988, of which three were removed for incubation. One of these was hatched under a broody hen and laboriously hand-reared; a duty shared by Peter Bircher, Gordon Campbell and Peter Small. The hatching was only the third in captivity in the world and the first in the UK. Since then other secretary birds have been hatched at Marwell, but all have had to be hand-reared.

Hand-rearing the first secretary bird bred in the UK.

Despite the Park's prime concern with larger mammals, it has an interest in native fauna. The British Herpetological Society approached Marwell to create a refuge for the breeding of sand lizards and natterjack toads, and suitable off-exhibit quarters were built to the specification of the project's

Television presenter, Chris Packham, and Paul Edgar on completion of the sand lizard enclosure.

co-ordinator, Paul Edgar. The sand lizards produced forty-three young in the first season and a remarkable 219 – a 93% hatch success rate – in the second year. The adults are kept in outside vivaria, but the youngsters are reared inside until large enough to stand a reasonable chance of survival, and are then released into suitable sites in the New Forest as agreed with the Forestry Commission. Tragedy struck in 1992 when vandals released some of the adult animals, which would probably not have fared well against birds and other predators in the Park. Despite the set back, the project continues, and the natterjack toads are now old enough to spawn.

In January 1990, violent storms caused more damage at Marwell than those of 1987. In addition to the loss of a number of trees and branches, the Przewalski horse house collapsed, and a large skylight in the giraffe house roof blew off and was never found! This time the power was off for three days, but emergency measures ensured that even the reptiles in the Education Centre survived. Less fortunate were three hog deer who died as the result of a tree falling in their enclosure. The loss of trees, even through natural causes, is regrettable, so many new trees have been planted in recent years to ensure that the ambience of the Park is preserved for future generations.

Important arrivals in 1990 were the golden-headed lion tamarins from Sau Paulo Zoo. Their status both in the wild and in captivity is more critical than that of their relations, the golden lion tamarins, whose record the Stud Book holder is aiming to emulate.

Golden-headed lion tamarin.

East African crowned cranes were hand-reared in 1990. Cranes are long-lived birds and it can take many years before they reach maturity and settle down to regular breeding. The first East African crowned cranes bred at Marwell was in 1984; the parents being survivors from the original importation when the Zoo opened. Sarus cranes now breed annually at Marwell, and it is hoped that the other two species in the collection, Stanley cranes and red-necked cranes, will eventually follow suit.

Despite the considerable, and time consuming, duties in operating the Zoo, John Knowles has not lost sight of the fact that Marwell is one small, but significant, part in the international conservation movement. This work takes him around the world as an ambassador for many animals and organisations, and he has served on the boards or committees of the British Joint Management of Species Group; the National Federation of Zoological Gardens of Great Britain and Ireland; the Zoological Society of

London; the Captive-Breeding Specialist Group of the Species Survival Commission; the International Species Information System; the International Union of Directors of Zoological Gardens; and the Whipsnade Wild Animal Park. Marwell is a member of the International Union for the Conservation of Nature and Natural Resources.

Marwell staff are active in national and international animal breeding programmes through the Joint Management of Species Committee of the European Species Survival Programmes (EEPs) and inter-continental programmes. In Britain, the Federation of Zoological Gardens of Great Britain and Ireland now oversee the management programmes for many groups of animals, and Marwell chairs four of these groups: Canids and Hyenas; Bovids; Pigs and Peccaries and, finally, Equids. Marwell also holds the International Stud Books for Grevy zebra and the Hartmann's mountain zebra.

In 1991 John Knowles was awarded the OBE for his services to conservation on the Queen's Birthday Honours' List.

The Children's Zoo, and later the Children's Farmyard, which was located along the South Road of the Zoo, were popular facilities, but they had little to offer apart from the opportunity for visitors to get closer to some animals. The need to develop this was long known, and led to the planning of Encounter Village. Encounter Village is being developed to illustrate the relationship between man and animal and, in particular, the story of domestication. The first phase was opened in the spring of 1992, and was fundamentally a farm yard area, initially accommodating goats, sheep and pot-bellied pigs, plus some more rather exotic domesticated animals, llama, camel and reindeer. New housing in 1993 permits a wider range of species to be kept. A rabbit mound allows children to obtain a rabbit's-eye view of the world, and animal-handling lectures and animal riding will enhance the educational potential of the Village. As funding becomes available, Encounter Village will expand.

Marwell sometimes receives animals from unexpected quarters. One morning the Southampton Port Authority telephoned to say that a muntjac deer had been found in the container port compound. It could possibly have swum in from the New Forest, but there was also a chance that it had come in a container and, as such, the animal would need to be quarantined. The arrival of the male was ideal, as Marwell had recently lost its male, leaving three females. Once out of quarantine the male was introduced to his new wives, and fawns are now due.

Young cotton-top tamarin.

Babirusa male.

In 1992 a trio of babirusa arrived. These small wild pigs from the island of Sulawesi in Indonesia are an endangered species that have seldom been kept in the UK. Marwell was fortunate in obtaining a female, with her juvenile daughter, and an unrelated male, via the Jersey Wildlife Preservation Trust. The only concern was that the male was an unproven breeder, however, this fear was dispelled when the older female produced twin piglets later in the year, and her daughter also, although she only reared one, the following year. A study is being made in Sulawesi to determine the wild status of these pigs, which required tracking the animals using radios. Attempts to design a pig-proof harness for the transmitters had not been successful so Marwell was consulted. A local saddler produced a prototype that was worn by Marwell's male for several months, and this model will hopefully fulfil its purpose in Indonesia.

In the twenty-one years since Marwell was first opened there have been many changes in the openness and responsibility of the Zoo community. There have been dramatic changes in international co-operation and involvement in the conservation issues that face our planet. John Knowles has played no small part in helping break down the barriers – perhaps it was because he was an 'outsider' when he first brought the tigers to Marwell, that people listened. The fact that progress has been made must not lead to complacency, because, for every success story, there are many waiting to happen. Marwell is increasingly aware of the need to take more animals on board the Ark, and to be able to offer further assistance with work in the field. Plans for the future will continue to be dependent upon the financial resources available – ultimately we are all able to help.